ERNEST SHACKLETON'S

IMPOSSIBLE ICE JOURNEY

CIARA O'NEAL

This one is for the very first captain of my ship. She was a brave leader who endured so much. Her time here was short, but she impacted so many. Love you, Mom.

Text © 2024 Ciara O'Neal
Illustration © 2024 L. Martin

Published by Orange Blossom Publishing
www.orangeblossombooks.com
info@orangeblossombooks.com

All rights reserved. No part of this publication may be reproduced, distributed, or transmitted in any form or by any means, including photocopying, recording, or other electronic or mechanical methods, without the prior written permission of the publisher, except in the case of brief quotations embodied in critical reviews and certain other noncommercial uses permitted by copyright law.

First edition: March 2025

Print ISBN: 978-1-949935-98-1
eBook ISBN: 978-1-949935-99-8
Library of Congress Control Number: 2024920647

Cover Design: L. Martin, Autumn Skye
Interior Formatting: Autumn Skye

Printed in the United States of America

CONTENTS

PREFACE	WHERE THE STORY STARTS	4
CHAPTER 1	PLAN. PACK. POLE!	6
CHAPTER 2	READY, SET, POLE!	11
CHAPTER 3	TRAPPED	14
CHAPTER 4	LITTLE HOPE FOR THE BOAT	22
CHAPTER 5	THE ENDURANCE TODAY	27

MORE ABOUT MY HERO, SIR ERNEST SHACKLETON 29

10 THINGS YOU DIDN'T KNOW ABOUT
    THE SHACKLETON EXPEDITION 32

ACKNOWLEDGEMENTS 34

ABOUT THE AUTHOR 35

PREFACE
WHERE THE STORY STARTS

See those guys over there? Yep. The ones using those fancy underwater robots. I bet they are patting themselves on the backs now that they found Ernest Shackleton's ship. They're the first humans to lay eyes on it in over 100 years.

THE ROBOTS USED TO FIND ERNEST'S SHACKLETON SUNKEN SHIP WERE ACTUALLY AUTONOMOUS UNDER-WATER VEHICLES. THAT'S A FANCY WAY OF SAYING NO ONE PILOTED THESE WATERBOTS. SCIENTISTS CONTROLLED THEM FROM FOUR MILES ABOVE MY HOME SWEET HOME. AND WHERE IS HOME, YOU MIGHT BE WONDERING?

My home, the South Pole. Now don't start picturing fluffy penguins skating across a pillow-like snow mound. I'll stop you right there. Getting to my neck of the woods is no easy task. That's why I am sure the humans on that boat are cheering now that they have spotted the sunken ship.

This expedition has all sorts of -*ists* on it like archeologists, glaciologists, geologists, etc. They're a bunch of scientists who are studying this or that.

Well, I hate to break it to you guys, but I was here first. Me, Sir E. Pincherton, the mysterious-but-good-looking lobster.

But we're getting ahead of ourselves, me thinks. All this interest in the South Pole didn't just begin. The race to the South Pole started back in the 1900s. (That's way before cell phones and video games, just so you know.) Explorers braved the everchanging dangers of the frigid Antarctic. One of those brave chaps was my personal hero, Sir Ernest Shackleton.

CHAPTER 1
PLAN. PACK. POLE!

Where is the most dangerous place on Earth? The Sahara, maybe, with its extreme temperature and no water in sight? Or Australia with its deadly creatures? Nope. None of these places. It's the Antarctic.

Not even the Arctic has the same number of dangers lurking just below the surface. The North Pole only has a few feet of ice floating in its waters. In the Antarctic, **glaciers** can go two miles deep! The land is covered in ice so heavy it digs into the ground.

Don't get me started on the weather. During the winter, the temperature falls below -100°F. Mind blown! Water freezes at 0°. Imagine 100 degrees colder than ice forming. Yikes. And the wind, it can blow over 200 miles per hour.

Into these dangers is exactly where explorers like Shackleton wanted to go, to the South Pole.

Shackleton wasn't the only captain who wanted to reach the South Pole. Adventurers from around the world scrambled to be the first to reach the mysterious, icy edge of the Earth. They sought the fame and glory that went with being an explorer during this time. These years, 1895-1922, were known as the "Heroic Age."

Explorers were treated like celebrities. Explorers wrote books and gave speeches. The king of England even knighted Shackleton after one of his expeditions! Fame and a thirst for adventure were enough to convince many men to face the trip. For those things, they would gladly face choppy waters filled with pointy pieces of ice and dangerously cold temperatures.

Many explorers tried and failed to reach the South Pole. Even Shackleton failed. Twice. The first time Shackleton traveled to the South Pole was 1901. But the explorers ran out of supplies 450 miles short of the South Pole. Shackleton also grew ill and had to return to England early.

Shackleton returned to the Antarctic in 1907. After landing on the icy shores, he and his crew trudged as far inland as they could. But they stopped ninety-seven miles short of the pole. You guessed it, they once again ran low on rations. A person's gotta eat, am I right? And it's not like they could go to the nearest grocery store.

Shackleton learned that his rival, Roald Amundsen, accomplished Shackleton's dream. Amundsen was the first man to reach the South Pole.

Shackleton was devastated. But he didn't give up. No, he dreamed bigger.

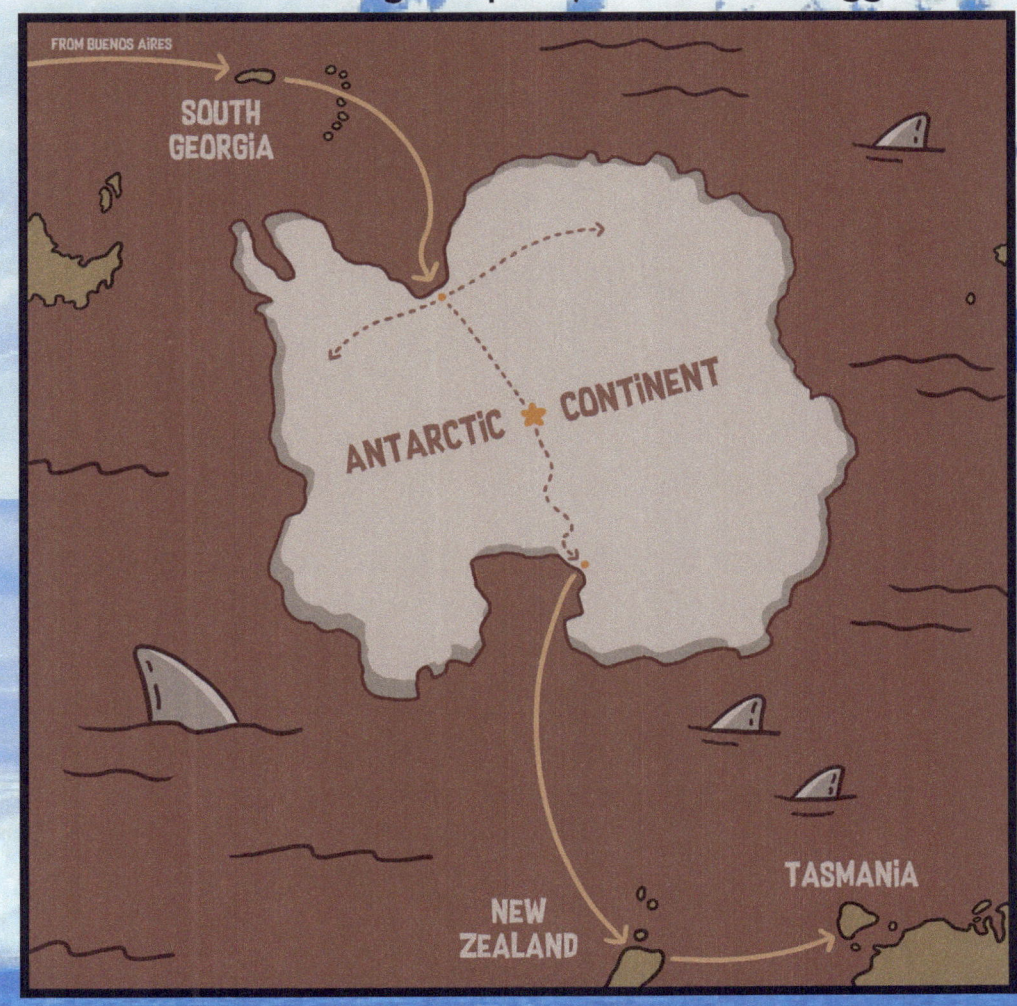

THIS BEAUTY WAS POWERED BY BOTH THE WIND AND AN ENGINE THAT BURNED COAL. AND LOOK AT THE TIP OF THAT SHIP! IT WAS OVER FOUR FEET THICK. THIS STURDY BOW HELPED THE ENDURANCE CUT THROUGH THE CHUNKS OF ICE FLOATING IN THE SEAS.

He would not only reach the South Pole, he would be the first to hike across the entire Antarctic by land.

To make this mission float, Shackleton needed a new boat. So he bought one and named it the *Endurance*. A trip to the South Pole would require the crew to keep going even when the journey became rough. Endurance fit.

Great leaders, like Shackleton, learn from their past mistakes. Remembering past mistakes, he problem-solved. For this transcontinental trip, Shackleton decided he didn't just need one vessel. He needed two. The first ship, the *Endurance*, would sail him across the Weddell Sea to get to Antarctic. Meanwhile, the second ship, full of supplies for the return hike, would wait on the other side of the continent.

Aside from carrying the crew and their sixty-nine sled dogs, the ships transported supplies. Below the deck, all sorts of essential items were stored like scientific equipment, rifles, lanterns, sleeping bags, and food. Coal was brought to power the motor. There were also three lifeboats just in case.

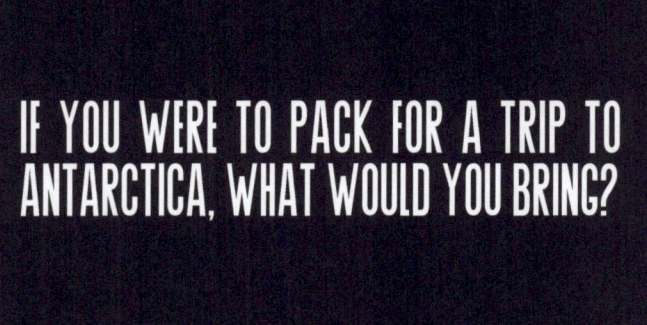

IF YOU WERE TO PACK FOR A TRIP TO ANTARCTICA, WHAT WOULD YOU BRING?

Shackleton's team planned to capture live penguins and seals. Not much was known about these animals in the 1900s. They wanted to study them. So they also brought tanks and cages. They packed a motorized sled called a sledge. It would carry the crew across the ice when they were no longer able to travel by boat.

Of course the ships carried plenty of food for the crew. They even had all the ingredients to make a mixture called sledge rations. It was a mix of oatmeal, beef protein, vegetable protein, salt, and sugar. When in solid form, it felt like cheese. But when boiled with water, it looked like pea soup. Sounds yummy, right? But at least it would keep the sailors from getting sick from malnutrition.

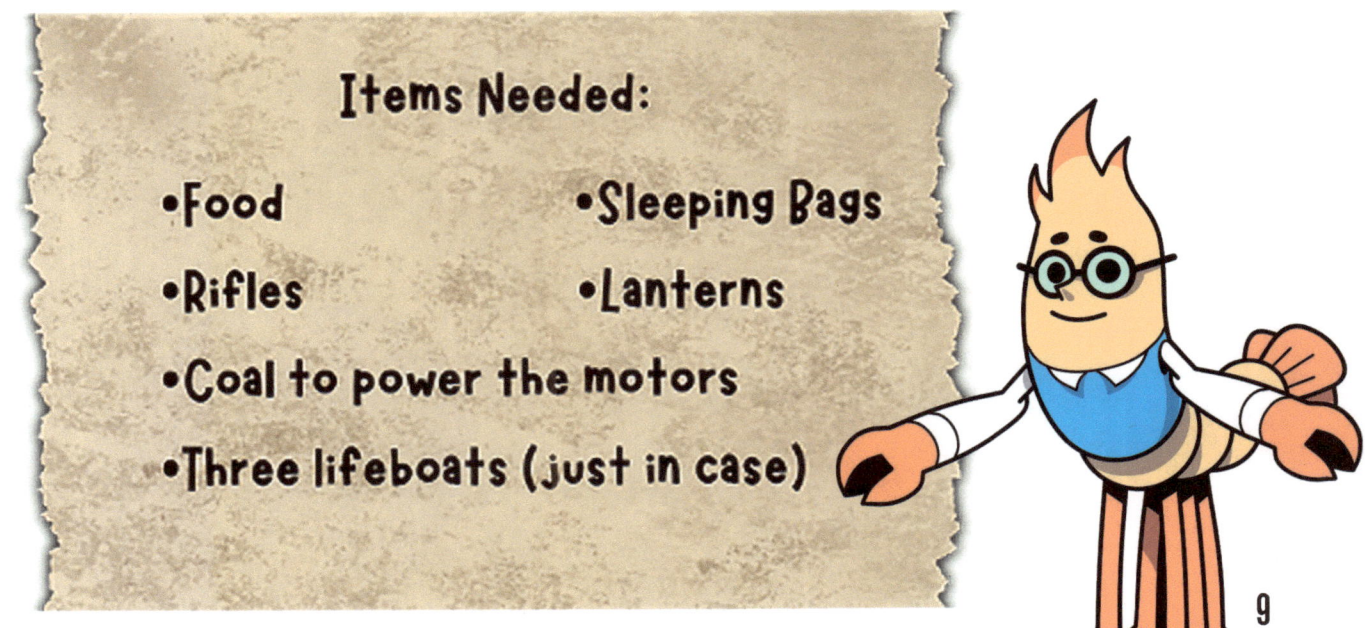

Items Needed:

- Food
- Sleeping Bags
- Rifles
- Lanterns
- Coal to power the motors
- Three lifeboats (just in case)

Shackleton wanted his men to be healthy and well-fed. So aside from sledge rations, *blech*, he kept canned meats, powdered milk and cocoa, vegetables, flour, and more.

He also stocked his ship with unexpected items like hockey skates, soccer balls, a banjo, a pool table, two pigs, and even a cat named Mrs. Chippy. He knew a happy crew would make getting through the hard times easier.

Over 5,000 men applied for jobs on Shackelton's ship. Only twenty-seven men were accepted. The hopeful heroes set sail from London, England, in 1914.

This journey was no vacation. Would being well prepared really make a difference? After all, the crew was headed to a place where ice was king.

SHACKLETON SOUGHT SAILORS WITH POLAR EXPERIENCE. BUT HE ALSO WANTED MEN WITH INTERESTING TALENTS LIKE SINGING.

NO BAD SINGERS RUINING THE BOSS'S SEA SHANTIES, THANK YOU VERY MUCH.

CHAPTER 2
READY, SET, POLE!

Shackleton heard just how cruel the ice could be at his last stop before sailing to the Antarctic. South Georgia was a small community on a tiny island. That island sat in the sea south of South America. I wasn't kidding about Shackleton going to the edge of the world!

While docked at South Georgia, other ship captains whispered warnings and rumors of rough seas and dangerously thick pack ice. Never had the captain seen such thick ice. A bad year for ice, the captains muttered over and over again.

But Shackleton had faith in his crew and his preparations. On December 5th, the crew of the *Endurance* left the known world behind.

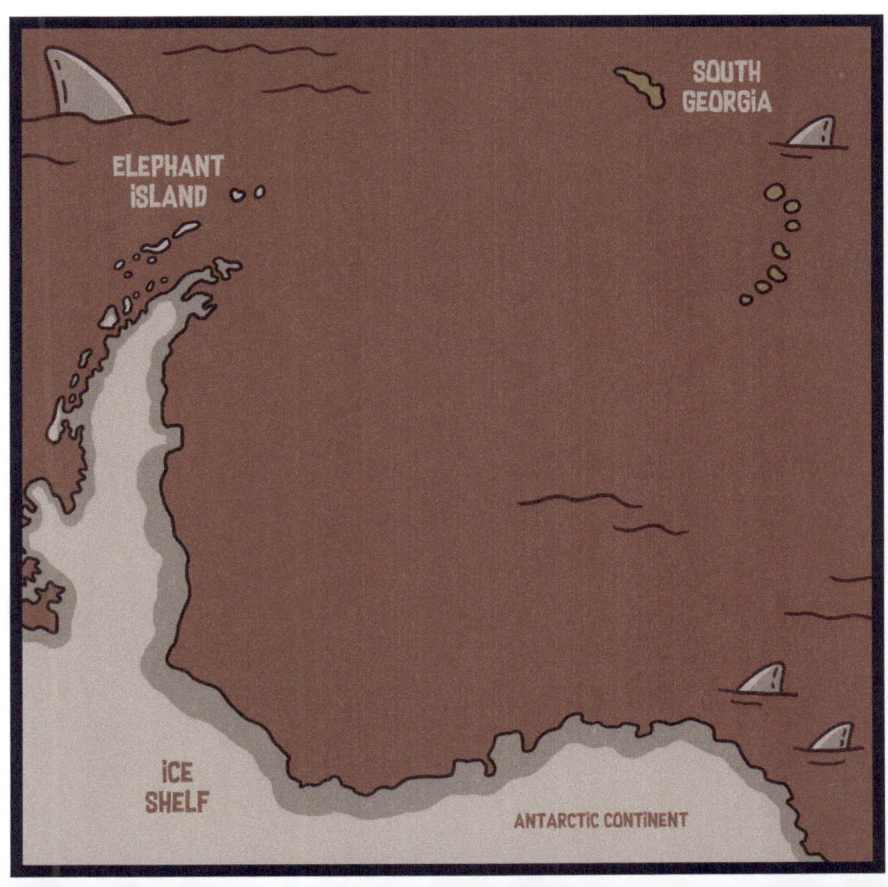

I BET YOU'RE WONDERING HOW IN THE WORLD THEY KNEW WHERE THEY WERE GOING. FRANK WORSLEY PLANNED THEIR PATH USING A TOOL CALLED A SEXTANT. HE PEERED DOWN THE TOOL TO MEASURE THE DISTANCE FROM THE HORIZON TO SOMETHING IN THE SKY—OBJECTS LIKE THE SUN OR A STAR.

Days after their departure, the *Endurance* discovered ice wasn't the only thing in the waters. Incredible animals, like myself, greeted the seamen as they traveled. Killer whales broke the surface nearby. All types of penguins slipped and slid closer to the boat especially when they heard the banjo.

Everyone was in high spirits. Christmas was coming. They sang carols and devoured a rare feast of turtle soup, minced pie, and fig-and-plum pudding. But as they floated further south the easy cheer couldn't last.

Each passing day, the *Endurance* carefully tiptoed through the minefield of ice. Monstrous chunks of ice, called growlers, scratched and scraped at the sides of the ship. Usually, growlers were never spotted this far north. 600 miles from the Antarctic shore, worry nipped at the crew. What would they find beyond the giant ring of pack ice that surrounded the Antarctic coast like walls around a castle?

The ocean became a maze. Openings in the ice became less and less. Frost blanketed everything from the rope to the deck. Sometimes the *Endurance* went the wrong direction searching for open paths in the ice. Other times, a frost fog drifted off the water and made it difficult for the crew to see.

The fog played tricks on the sailors' eyes. Identifying the real dangers was crucial because the sailors passed hundreds of icebergs each day. It became very difficult to tell the difference between real glaciers and mirages. Being able to identify the real icy danger was essential. Sometimes, the sailors passed over 400 bergs each day.

Some days, the *Endurance* encountered ice so thick they couldn't move in any direction. One such day happened on New Year's Day. The crew sang *Auld Lang Syne*. Even the dogs joined in with high pitched howls.

Types of Ice	Shackleton and his men faced many types of ice. Each kind posed a different danger.		
	Icebergs	Ice Floes	Pack Ice
	Pieces of glaciers that have broken off of the larger mass	Giant, mostly flat sheets of ice that are sixty feet or more across	Giant and smaller pieces of floating ice that squeeze together to form a massive group

CHAPTER 3
TRAPPED

Sixty miles from the Antarctic shore, a massive storm slammed into the boat. Using an iceberg as a shield, the crew tried to escape the raging winds. But the storm mashed the pack ice around the ship, squeezing so tightly that the *Endurance* became trapped in the ice's clutches.

In good weather, they were only a day's sailing away from where they wanted to land. But this was not good weather. And matters were growing worse—the giant sheet of pack ice holding the *Endurance* prisoner was floating north. The opposite direction of where they wanted to go!

ONE OF THE CREW MEMBERS COMPARED THE BOAT TO "AN ALMOND IN THE MIDDLE OF A CANDY BAR." HE WAS FACING A BAD SITUATION WITH A POSITIVE ATTITUDE. HAVE YOU EVER BEEN THROUGH A HARD TIME WHERE YOU NEEDED TO STAY POSITIVE TO GET THROUGH IT?

Shackleton's crew dig around the *Endurance*. They try to free the boat from the pack ice.

WEEKS OF WAITING

Shackleton needed a plan. Perhaps the crew could dig the ship out? Setting to work, the sailors used pick axes and saws. They chipped, hacked, and cut ice around the boat. But after days of battling, they only gained a few feet and...exhausted themselves.

The end of winter would bring warmer weather and waters. Shackleton hoped the *Endurance* would break free from the ice in the spring. So the crew hunkered down and prepared to wait out the winter.

The crew accepted this delay with good humor. Being stuck in the ice was something they would overcome. They were so close to landing on Antarctica, they could not give up now.

With no sailing to be done, a new routine began…a schedule filled with chores. Oh man! Sailors scrubbed the deck and melted ice to drink (which was way harder than it sounds). Others hunted seals or peeled potatoes. The men grumbled about the work. Who wouldn't complain? But they soon settled in.

But the most challenging thing about life on the floe wasn't the extreme temperatures or chores. Nope. It was boredom. The men had to be creative to find fun. Some sailors built dog kennels on the ice floe. They called them "dogloos."

Others played rowdy games of soccer, and hockey echoed across the ice floe. A daring photographer climbed the mast to capture photos.

Some sailors sought excitement by participating in dog sled races, card games, and haircut tournaments. None of the crew were barbers. But that didn't stop them from challenging each other to see who could give the best haircut. Man, would I hate to be the guy who had the losing barber cutting my hair.

But as time ticked on, it became harder to stay positive. The ship's creaks and groans were horrible reminders of the extreme pressure the boat faced as ice pressed in on all sides. What if it snapped under all that pressure? What would they do stranded at the edge of the world with no way home?

Days stuck in the ice turned to weeks. And weeks melted into months. September began the Antarctic spring. Food ran low. And so did the men's patience.

Shackleton's men built a dog race track. They even bet chocolate and other items on who would win. I'd bet two pieces of chocolate for Shakespeare to beat Samson!

They spoke of plans for the future. Many never wanted to see a scrap of ice ever again. Everyone eagerly awaited freedom from the ice's crippling claws.

Every now and then, spots of ice surrounding the ship cracked. A peek of hope. But no openings were large enough to fit the ship. It would be soon, the men thought.

Without warning…a giant ice floe crashed in the ice where the *Endurance* was trapped. The ice quaked. Pinned from all sides, the ship groaned under the pressure. Leaks sprouted. The crew took turns pumping water out of the boat around the clock. Would it be enough to save the ship from sinking?

The piles of ice eight feet and taller surrounding the ship grew. Frantically, the crew shoveled ice away from the walls. Others kept pumping water.

The tortured wood of the *Endurance* howled. Millions of tons of pressure shoved against its sides. Piles of ice crowded the ship. Frantically, the crew shoveled ice away from the walls. Other members kept pumping water.

Nothing could relieve the pressure. Nothing could save their ship.

In late evening on October 25, 1915, an enormous CRACK ripped through the air. It was the end of the *Endurance*.

THE MEN HAD TO CHOOSE ONLY THE THINGS THAT WOULD WEIGH THEM DOWN THE LEAST. THE PHOTOGRAPHER, WORLEY, HAD OVER 400 GLASS SLIDES THAT HELD HIS PICTURES. HE ENDED UP BREAKING OR LEAVING OVER 200 BEHIND.

The wreckage of *Endurance* as it sinks to its final resting place.

The crew rushed to unload what they could. Left behind were the comforts and games. Dismay flooded the crew as the ship's mast snapped and the boat's boards twisted and broke. But the worst sight, the miles and miles of ice stretching in all directions.

That night, they drew straws to see who would use a sleeping bag. With only eighteen bags, the other ten men had to make due with woolen blankets. And one poor sailor grew sick with snow blindness—a temporary illness that caused a traveler to go blind because of the glare of the sun off the snow.

While stuck, the crew had drifted 1,000 miles off course. They were stranded with no way to call for help. It might seem hopeless, but don't count Shackleton out just yet.

The next morning, Shackleton had a plan. They would drag two of the life boats across the ice until they reached open water. After that, they would sail to a re-supply station on Paulet Island 346 miles away.

Let's pause for a moment and remind ourselves about where the most dangerous place on Earth is, shall we? Yup. You remember correctly, Antarctica. The place our brave explorers are trekking on foot.

HAVE NO FEAR. THERE HAVE BEEN NO ACTUAL KILLER WHALE ATTACKS ON HUMANS EVER. BUT SEALS AND PENGUINS AREN'T AS LUCKY.

The Antarctic contains 90% of the world's snow and ice. Temperatures almost never rise above freezing. Cracks in the ice waited to dump unsuspecting sailors into icy waters. The crew feared that killer whales would mistake an unlucky seamen for a seal. Add to that hurricane-strength winds and dwindling food shortages. The chances of our daring crew surviving dropped like the temperature around them.

For seven grueling days the crew trudged across the ice. The hike was difficult and very slow. To cross the length of a football field took them nearly two-and-a-half hours.

Even though the weather warmed, the sailors weren't safe. The ice grew unpredicatable. But that didn't mean that it was safe for the sailors. One day, a crack erupted between the crew and the lifeboats. The men risked their lives to retrieve them. After seven days, they only slogged seven miles! There were at least 300 miles to reach the supply station. Could the crew survive the trip?

The crew set up a camp.

Shackleton called a halt. There was nothing else to do but wait for the ice floe to drift into open water. Shackleton's men set up a camp they called "Patience Camp."

Many sailors shared the few tents left. But being crammed together like sardines was the least of their problems. It was difficult to bathe in the freezing landscape, let alone find drinkable water. The men ate mostly seal and penguin meat. They stayed on high alert after a giant leopard seal jumped out of the water and tried to attack a sailor.

No one played pranks or silly games any more. The men spent their time reading and standing watch. Endless days with nothing to do but stare across the endless ice pushed the men's limits. Many wondered if they would ever see dry land or their families again.

LAND HO!

It took four months of slow drifting, but in April, land ho! The men cheered. Elephant Island came into view.

But as they broke camp, their ice floe cracked and crumbled under their feet. The crew rushed to the lifeboats. Now they faced a new enemy, the open ocean. Icy water splashed into the boat, soaking the freezing men. Wind and waves tossed the boat like a toy in the heavy storms.

Half the crew suffered from seasickness. The other half were out of their minds with dysentery, an infection that caused high fever, cramping, and diarrhea. Everyone was dehydrated. Their tongues became so swollen they couldn't swallow food.

Battling the raging seas kept the men awake day and night. They rowed and rowed. Seven days later, they reached Elephant Island.

Their adventure was far from over. This was not the re-supply station. In fact, Elephant Island was hardly more than a large rock.

AFTER 497 DAYS, THE MEN STOOD ON SOLID GROUND ONCE MORE.

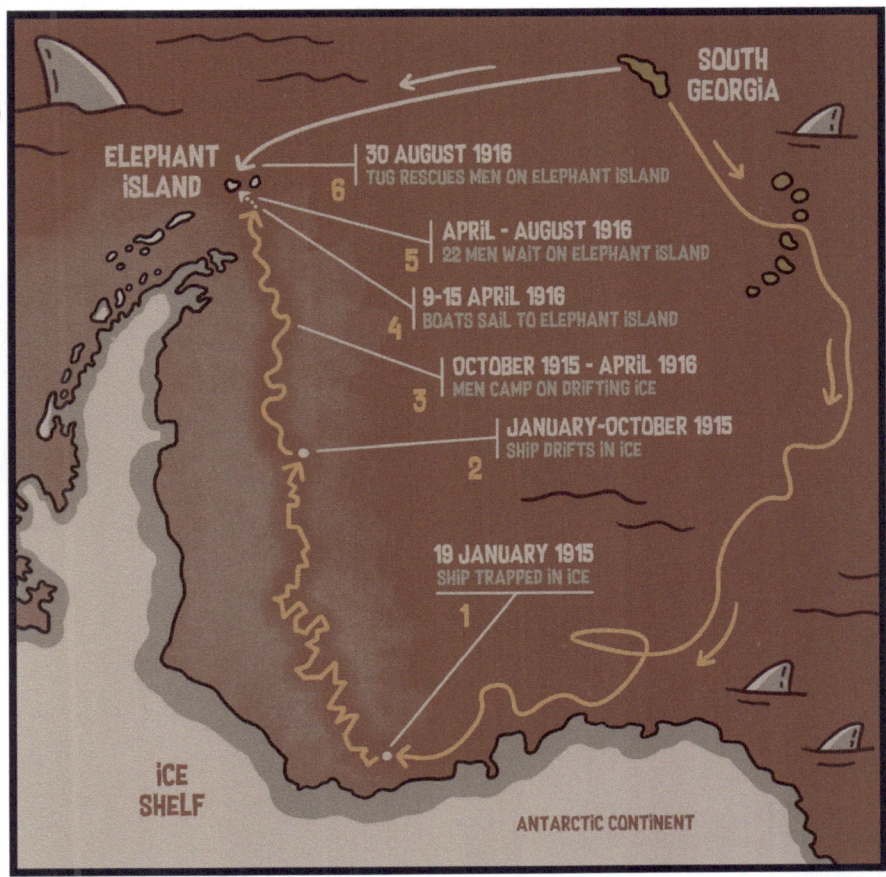

CHAPTER 4
LITTLE HOPE FOR THE BOAT

Shackleton knew the chances of being rescued were low. No one lived on Elephant Island for a reason. It was cold, rocky, and had absolutely no resources.

After nine days of rest, Shackleton prepared to leave for help. He knew his sickly, starving crew could not survive another voyage. Shackleton selected five men to travel with him. These five would brave the perilous waters that stretched between Elephant Island and South Georgia. They alone would search for help that was over 800 miles away.

Wait a minute. Let's review that plan: that's an 800-mile journey on a teeny tiny boat with no sails, no motor, just paddles. The men wore holey clothes and had few supplies. I have the same questions. Could they really survive the open ocean? But what hope did the crew have if Shackleton didn't go?

Shackleton's life boat battled giant waves. The men bailed water and shivered in the cold wind. Days passed. Water slammed the sailors. Cold crept in. But they endured.

On the 16th day, the shores of South Georgia appeared in the distance. But like a cruel trick a huge storm whipped up. It didn't die down until the next day.

When Shackleton's men stepped ashore, they were desperate for water and rest. Their exhaustion was so great, they could hardly pull the boat out of the water. Getting the boat ashore was the least of their problems. They had landed on the wrong side of the South Georgia island.

The only way to reach the supply station was a dangerous trek through a mountain range.

Normally, no one ventured far from the shores of South Georgia island. And for good reason. There was no way past the sheer mountain walls, incredibly tall peaks, and the slippery glaciers that dropped into deep holes in the ice.

Leaving behind as much gear as possible, he prepared to cross land no else braved. Shackleton and the men able to continue removed screws from the life boat. They pushed them through the soles of their boots. This upgrade kept them from slipping on the ice. They packed three days of food and water and set out.

Their first obstacle? A narrow ridge. Step by slow step, they conquered the ridge. A wall of mountain and a slippery climb down a glacier lay ahead. But neither of these landforms were nearly as dangerous as the coming nightfall.

Leaving the tent and sleeping bags behind allowed the men to move more quickly. But their tattered clothes provided little protection the dropping temperatures. Getting caught this high up could be deadly. Speeding their steps, they raced the moon to a valley. The men could not be caught high up in the mountain once night fell. The temperatures would drop to deadly lows. Speeding their steps along, they made it to the valley. From there, the moon led them through. Until at last, they arrived at a glacier.

Disappointment crashed through the group. This was not the city. It was the Fortuna Glacier. The ice blocked their path. After twenty-four hours of hiking, sleep called to them. But they could not stop or they may never wake again. The men backtracked.

Shackleton and his men took one exhausted step after another. For hours. Suddenly, there was a gap. The men followed the rocky path. Up they climbed. And there! Twelve miles in the distance stood South Georgia.

Covering the miles as quickly as possible, Shackleton and his men tumbled into the settlement. The people of South Georgia were shocked to see them. No one came from that direction ever. Let alone dirty men with matted hair and beards.

The city manager didn't recognize the captain who had set sail from South Georgia months before. Shortly after telling his story, Shackleton focused on rescuing his crew from Elephant Island. His second-in-command went to retrieve the sick sailors on the other side of the island.

Rescuing the twenty-two men on Elephant Island proved to be just as difficult as every other part of this terrible journey. Shackleton borrowed a ship three days after arriving in South Georgia. This boat met an unbreakable wall of pack ice sixty miles from Elephant Island. Shackleton had to turn back.

But he didn't give up. The Uruguayan government wanted to help. They lent Shackleton a second ship. This time, Shackleton sailed even closer to his stranded sailors. But the ice stopped the boat 100 miles from Elephant Island.

The pack ice also squashed Shackleton's third try at rescuing his crew. The tiny boat, named *Emma*, was defeated by the pack ice.

The men called their boat house "The Snuggery". They weren't wrong. It does look rather snug.

Meanwhile, the men on Elephant Island struggled to stay hopeful. They'd built flimsy shelters out of the life boats. And they hunted seals and penguin for their meals.

Shackleton had been gone over four months. Every day, Shackleton's second-in-command, Frank Wild, told the sailors that today might be the day the captain returned. So many times before, he had been wrong. Many of the men wondered if Wild would ever be right.

Shackleton didn't let the last three failures stop him. His men needed him. Shackleton convinced the Chilean government to join forces with him. The weather and waters favored the powerful little steamer called *Yelcho*.

127 days after Shackleton left Elephant Island, he finally made it to his crew.

All twenty-eight members boarded the boat going home to England. But not the *Endurance*. For 106 years it has rested in the icy waters off the Antarctic. And I suppose that is where my story begins.

CHAPTER 5
THE ENDURANCE TODAY

You humans are a curious bunch. But it's been a long time since I have seen any of you around here. I mean who really wants to battle ever-moving ice, blizzards, and temperatures dipping below zero degrees Fahrenheit? Okay, maybe discovering Shackleton's boat after 100 years would be one of the most amazing discoveries of all time.

At first, scientists from all over the world arrived on a huge ice-breaking boat called *Agulhas II*. For over two weeks, they sent underwater cameras 10,000 feet below to scour the sea floor. It was one of the best games of hide-and-seek I've ever played. (I am pretty sure I held the title for hide-and-seek champion until these pesky scientists arrived. You're next, Big Foot. Just wait, I'll reclaim my title!)

Finally, the scientists found the sunken ship. (I mean, it took you long enough.) I'm sure they expected to encounter important pieces of history. And yes, the cold water has kept the ship in tip-top shape. The *Endurance*'s wood has barely decayed.

I let the crew of the *Agulhas II* around. I mean it's not like I haven't explored every nook and cranny already. Many pieces of the wreckage are completely whole, like the ship's steering wheel. The ship is still upright. And even the carved name *Endurance* is still clearly visible on the side of the ship.

But I betcha the scientists got more of an eyeful than they ever bargained for! Covering Shackleton's ship were sea stars, sea anemones, and sea squirts. And no, I'm not being mean, they really are called squirts. Look, here's a picture if you don't believe me.

I know I came as quite a surprise to them. I, Sir E. Pincherton, am a brand-new species of lobster no one has ever seen before. That's right, people, admire my incredible crustaceous self.

I guess you could say that once the old crew headed out, a new crew came in! But don't worry, boss, I will take good care of her.

MORE ABOUT MY HERO, SIR ERNEST SHACKLETON

Ernest Shackleton was born in Ireland on February 15, 1874. He was the second of ten children. Shackleton devoured books. He craved adventure like some people crave gold or fame. His father hoped that Shackleton would follow in his footsteps and become a doctor. But adventure was in Shackleton's blood from the moment he could open a book, and nothing short of a job filled with excitement and danger would do.

By age twenty, Shackleton was moving up the ranks aboard ships. First, he earned the rank of second mate, or third in command of a ship. Later, he moved up to first mate. A first mate only answers to a captain. At age twenty-four, he became a master mariner. That meant he could be a captain of any British ship.

Shackleton's thirst for adventure lured him to the South Pole. His first exploration was aboard a ship led by Robert Falcon Scott. Even though

Shackleton desperately wanted to be there, he grew sick before the expedition ended and was sent home.

His second attempt to reach it fell short by 112 miles, but Shackleton was knighted. Being famous didn't satisfy Shackleton. He had to return to Antarctica. It sung a siren's song to him. Even with his failure with the *Endurance,* he planned another trip to the Pole.

Sadly, Shackleton's pursuit of adventure was never quite enough to take him all the way to the South Pole. He died of heart failure on South Georgia Island just before he could leave on his last voyage.

Shackleton will always be thought of as one of the greatest leaders of all times. Despite all odds, he kept his crew together and brought them back to safety. History will remember a man that cared greatly for his crew, putting himself into dangerous situations to make sure every last man made it home. His endurance will always be admired especially by Sir E. Pincherton and this author.

MAPS

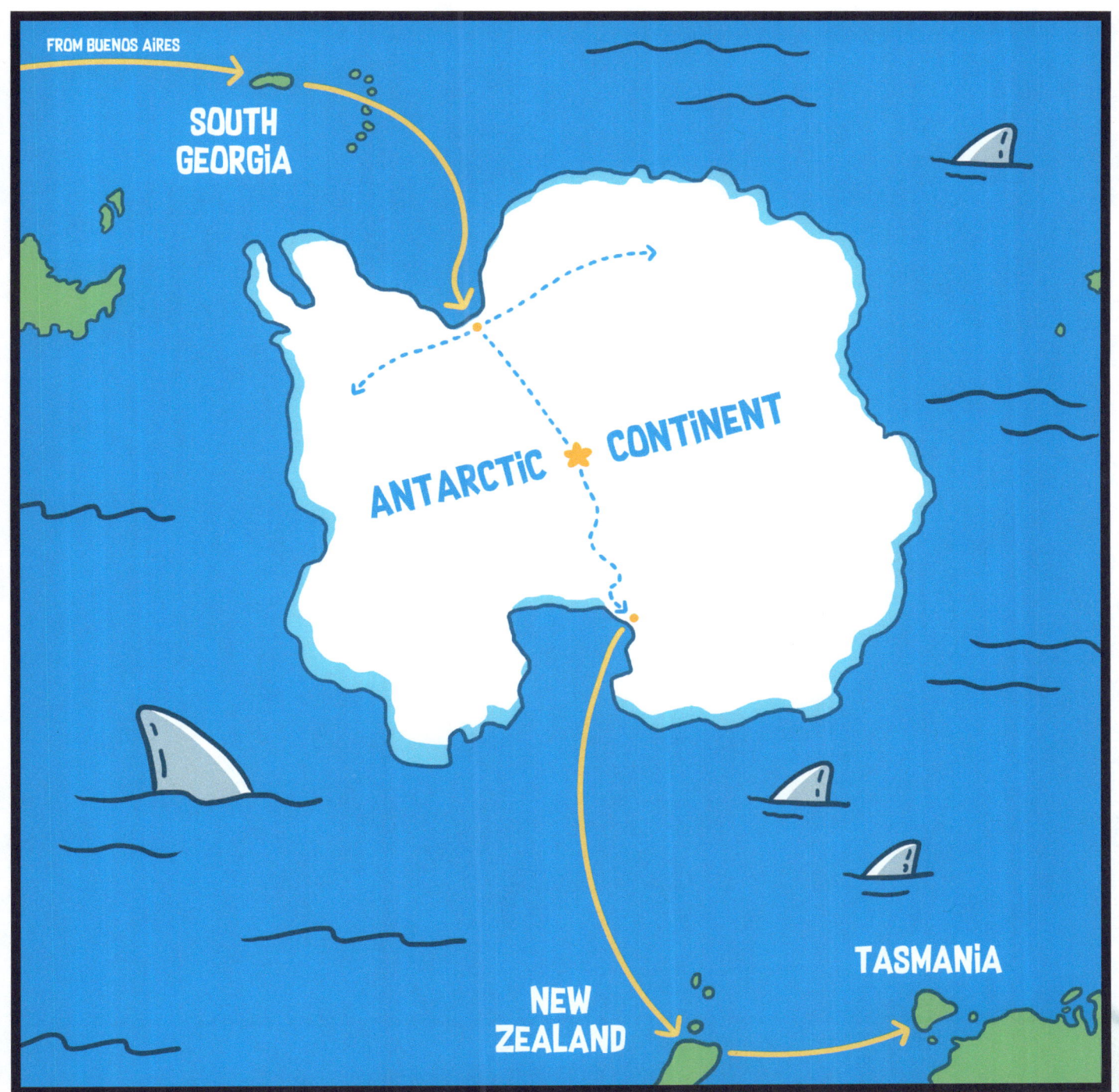

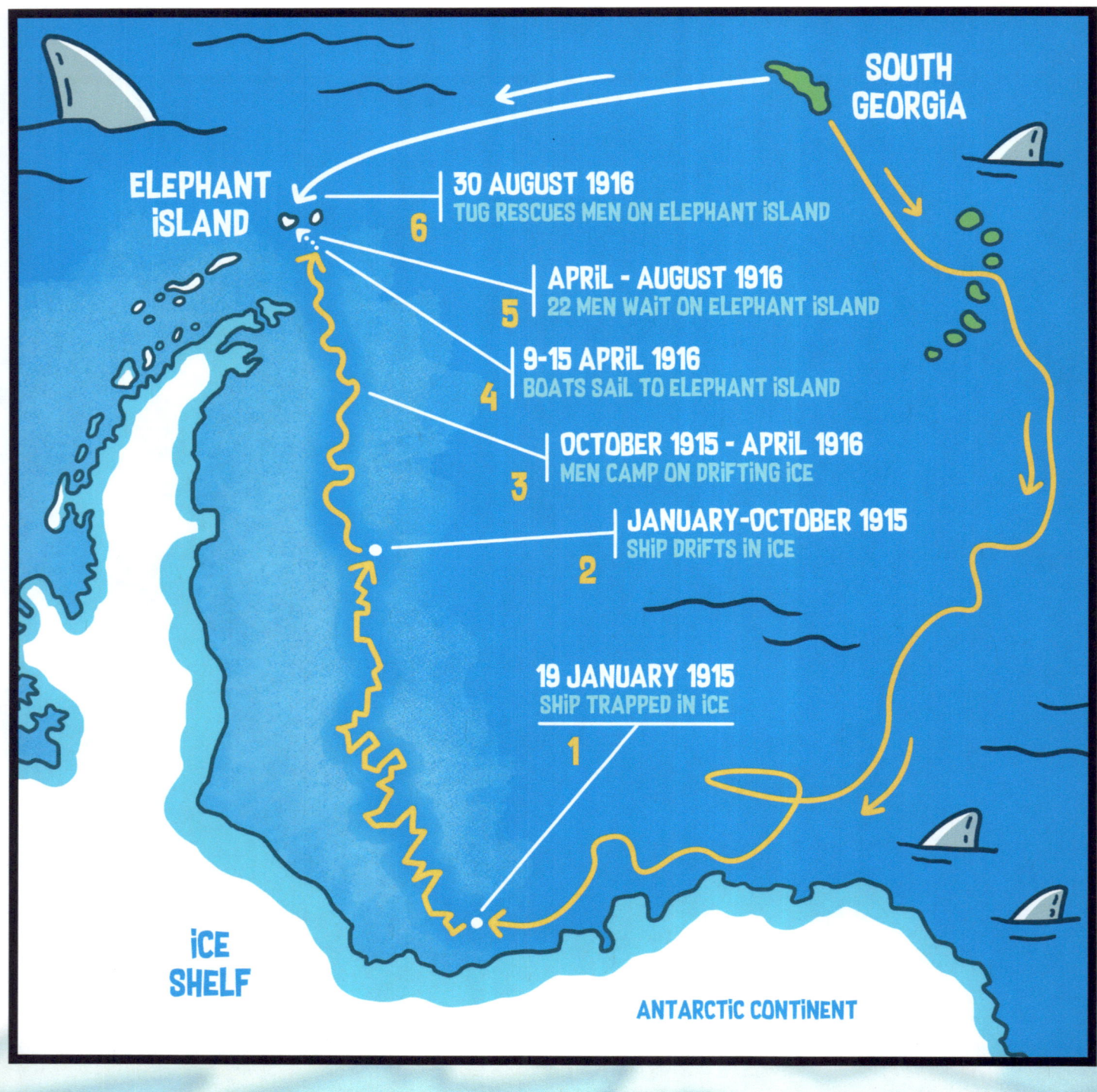

10 THINGS YOU DIDN'T KNOW ABOUT THE SHACKLETON EXPEDITION

1. The Endurance was quite the tourist attraction before it left the docks back in England. Sightseers flocked to the port to see the daring crew.

2. Queen Alexandra inspected the boat before it set sail. She even gifted Shackleton with a Bible.

3. The Endurance had a stowaway! Percy Blackborrow hid until the ship was so far away, it couldn't turn around. When he revealed himself to the captain, Shackleton was furious. But after Shackleton joked that if the crew got too hungry, he might be supper, he gave the young man a job as the ship's steward.

4. For part of the year, the sun shone all day and all night. In other months, there was nonstop darkness.

5. The crew loved to pull pranks on each other. On one occasion, the crew convinced one crewman that everyone was going to have a costume party at the next port. The seaman showed up dressed up in a bedsheet and a tea kettle for a hat. Unfortunately for him, he was the only one in costume.

6. Mrs. Chippy, despite the name, was actually a male cat.

7. The Antarctic wildlife was not afraid of humans. The animals had never seen humans before. The crew could walk up to, pet, and even pick up penguins.

8. Crew member Orde-Lees used a bike and practiced tricks on the ice.

9. The sunken *Endurance* was discovered 100 years to the day that Shackleton died.

10. Nowadays, many tourist companies offer hikes and cruises to follow the path of Shackleton's terrible trek to reach the South Georgia community. The trip is much safer and more luxurious.

ACKNOWLEDGEMENTS

There are so many people to thank after writing a book. First off, we should thank those explorers who were brave enough to go beyond the known and strong enough to stay committed to what they believe in.

Also, a huge thank you to my publisher who believed that I could make this book happen. And finally, my beautiful critique partners who have been my sisters every step of the way.

ABOUT THE AUTHOR

Ciara O'Neal's own thirst for adventure has taken her to many places in the world. But she still thinks some of the best adventures are the ones found in books. That's why she's busy peddling books to every middle school student who steps foot in her library. If you can't find her there, she's most likely chasing yellow buggies and runaway mermaids.

www.ingramcontent.com/pod-product-compliance
Lightning Source LLC
Chambersburg PA
CBHW041530070526
44586CB00002B/28